BETWEEN
TWO FIRES

John Grey

Cyberwit.net
HIG 45 Kaushambi Kunj, Kalindipuram
Allahabad - 211011 (U.P.) India
http://www.cyberwit.net
Tel: +(91) 9415091004
E-mail: info@cyberwit.net

Printed at Quarterfold Printabilities.

Contents

Poetry Lesson 1 7

The Hurt Does Not Inspire Me To Write 8

The Voices 9

To My Heir 10

His Floaters 11

Between Two Fires 12

The End Of A Perfect Relationship 14

After The Forest Fire 15

A Man's Sleep Is No Longer His Castle 17

Biomath 19

My Complain Department 20

Regarding The Woman Across The Street 22

He Falls In Love With A Painting 24

Welcome To The Whitehorse Inn 25

Refugees 26

October On Broad Street 27

In My Dream 29

From Deep In The Bowels Of Suburbia 31

A Boy At The Wake 33

Louisiana Childhood 35

The Pleasure 37

Bathers 38

The Mississippi Above New Orleans 39

Emma 41

Intruder In The Mist 42

The Rounds 43

An Education In The Northern Woods 45

The Loneliest Man In The World 48

Passive Anger 49

The Phony Thaw 51

Between The Woman And The Telemarketer 52

The Farm-Woman 54

Dream Woman/Dream Man 56

The Crystal Horse 58

My Connection 60

Catalogues 62

On The Walk To Marge's After Henry's Death 64

The Artist In The Moment 66

Looking West From My Sister's Property In Emerald 67

The Bet 68

Those Times She Really Does Need You 70

With An Ex, This Is As Good As It Gets 72

Coincidentally 73

My First And Last Time Hunting 75

Dirge 77

The Map Man 78

Newspapers 80

Children Lost In The Woods 82

The Other Person 83

Abduction 85

The Dead Of Oz 86

Welcome To The Natural World 87

People Are No Good 88

Regarding Love 90

Ella 91

Frogs 92

A Trial Separation On Trial 94

Splendor 96

The Future Of Literature 97

Poetry Lesson 1

a poem is words
arranged in such away
so as not to be
financially
viable

The Hurt Does Not Inspire Me To Write

Sorrow is nothing more
than drool from an old man's mouth,
a flattened squirrel in the road,
a house after a fire,
a padlock on a playground gate.

Yes it writes mawkish poetry.
But it hasn't the stamina for a novel.
Nor enough rapport with color
to make it onto canvas.

I first encountered sorrow
as an unfulfilled need.
I was a baby at the time.
I screamed the paint off my crib.

Since then
it has spread its doleful wings
but, under the surface,
is no more sophisticated
than that bawling child.

To be honest,
I prefer boredom
as a source of inspiration.
It has no prejudices.
It doesn't prejudge.
And I don't have to hear it
from that wailing kid in me.

The Voices

I'm growing older,
yet I'm here with some younger words.
A few have traveled a long way
from the last time they were spoken.

I can't hear my father
but my mother, my sisters,
are as clear as night sky's constellations.
Same as my childhood nursery rhymes,
school slang, the clatter of adding machines
in the bank back office where I first worked.
And the shapeless, invigorating buzz
of downtown strangers as they crowd
the footpaths, and the whoosh of
air-conditioning as store doors swing open.

Memory is a half-opened window pane,
where eucalyptus trees wallow
in fresh south-easterlies,
lizards stir, toads plop, sulphur-cockatoos shriek.

And it's such a relief,
and full of sounds and voices.
What a respite from my usual thoughts.
I hear others.
I don't have to listen to myself.

To My Heir

I was hoping to gift you
the woods and wildlife,
not a scarred, barbed forest
and those mysterious dead fish.

And a village of course
with all buildings intact,
a modest economy
that comforts and feeds.

I actually had faith that peace
was more than just a word in the dictionary.
But all the white doves can do
is shrug their feathery shoulders.

The olive tree can't be accounted for
let alone its branches.
And words refuse to be taken back.
So your inheritance is soldiers,

explosions, airplanes overhead.
Go on, indict my generation.
Put the blame where it fidgets
and turns its eyes away from you.

His Floaters

Every time
he opens his eyes,

right there in the vitreous,
a game is being played
with random black dots.

All he wants is vision,
clear, unadulterated,
but he shares what he can see
with some video game
from way back in the
early 1980's.

It's like Pong
but without the paddles.

And all his eye doctor can say is,
"With any luck,
in time they'll fade."

Sure, the doc can be optimistic.,
But he's not the one who's keeping score.

Between Two Fires

Enemy and friend of mankind .
Like my ex-wife, I suppose.
Or the blazing history of the house
next door fueling my twelve-year-old face
with the buzz of an irrational
jitterbugging light and heat
and the fireplace that warmed us,
welded us into one family unit,
flame grinning like our faces,
strong, purifying as a parent's touch.
I understand the cruelty now
of that charred walk
through such elementary forces
as tears, disgust and dread.
Understand the basic matter
of creation latching onto
sofas, cushions and relationships.
And my ex-wife rears her duality
again in the kindling of my memory,
the good crackle of the
simple sacrifices of love,
the pagan fire-worship of our anger.
And that house next door
became the forests above our town
as the fear swept through us
even fiercer than black wind
and the hearth opened its yawning
hot mouth to intelligence,
to tales of Apollo, Helios, Hestia,

Loki and a pantheon of fire gods.
And what it is in these letters
from Teresa but the flicker
of fire, that form of divinity
and the charred edge of fire,
power punishing itself,
orange and relentless.

The End Of A Perfect Relationship

Laura is no longer your Laura.
Those days are passed.
The togetherness that brought the rest of us
to the very edge of jealousy
is no more.
Without the comparison,
we're more content in our own flawed relationships.
Now we see you as one person
And Laura is one too.
We don't automatically invoke the term,
the two of you.

Even textbook combinations can diverge, break apart.
We've seen it with our own eyes.
We try not to treat either of you differently
but it isn't easy.
Ask a question and we still expect two voices, one answer.
But the responses are so solitary.
We have to ask the question separately.

Even time has a different way of passing.
We no longer think in blocks of it,
like the twenty years you were a couple.
Now we see you and Laura in terms of days apart.

Perhaps, you'll find another.
So might Laura.
But there aren't enough hours of love left
to come anywhere near two decades.
Meanwhile, the rest of us work with what we have.
It's been better since perfection took the fall.

After The Forest Fire

Hours after the fire went out,
and the dust settled
like small town people after dark,
and smoke became air,
and breeze gave back
the good breathing that flames stole,

the people returned to see what was left,
to sift through ashes, scour rubble
for the sense of ever having lived there,
stepped over charred beams, scorched tiles,
melted cups and saucers,
and the heat that remained
was almost apologetic
as someone picked up a ring
and tossed it back down again
or was blistered by an armless china doll.

So many eyes burned like their houses did,
neither bitter nor penitent
nor sorrowful nor angry,
but red and raw with a kind of awe,
full of the worst that can happen's
amplitude of hope,
like encountering the home of their dreams
in the burnt-out husk of the old one -
more rooms, fancier filigree,
maybe solid brick instead of flammable wood.

No one was the person they were -
they were who they needed to be
to get on with the rebuilding.
They stood in that gutted landscape
like farmers who have just razed a stand of forest
and are eager to furrow, to plant seed.

It was not a tribute to human strength,
more a passing nod to the benefits of frailty.
A good wife dies.
You're shocked. You mourn.
Then you marry her prettier sister.

A Man's Sleep Is No Longer His Castle

Every morning,
I'm provided with
an update on my prior night's sleep.

It's not something I require.
Nor did I ever ask for it.

But she tallies up the snores anyway.
As she does, the kicking feet,
the swinging hands,
and how many times I roll over.

It's the talking that
really intrigues her.
Mostly I'm speaking in dream tongues
but, occasionally, something lucid
will emerge from my lips.

Last night, so she tells me,
I spoke the name "Veronica,"
not once but three times.

This is one of those occasions
when I must respond
to the list she has prepared for me.

There are a series of multiple choice questions
posed by this certain look in her eye.

Who was Veronica?
a/ A slut who did it with everyone
b/ Some virginal princess I was hot on but couldn't
make headway with.

Apart from a heightening of her glare factor,
the alternatives for "Who is Veronica?"
are roughly the same.

Biomath

Forget the Math book,
I asked the leaf mold
if A=B + C.

Not expecting an answer.

The veins perfectly divided,
light through treetops multiplied,

but only touch and myopia
could add worth a damn.

I bent down to smell,
surrounded myself in expressions.

At the crisscross of the numbers,
I inhaled.

Subtraction.
Breath took my breath away.

My Complain Department

My older brother would tag along
after my sadness.
He'd watch me stuff my head in the pillow,
scratch at the blankets, squeeze the sheets
together like the pimple on my chin.
"What have you got to complain about,"
was his favorite saying.

I'd take a swipe at him.
It was house money. At best,
I'd connect with his silly jaw.
At worst, he'd grab me by the arms
and hold me until my spit subsided.
Then we'd laugh.
He was right.
Teenage girls, acne, and algebra -
the unholy trio were cut down
by their own absurdity.

He was a farter par excellence
and the sneakiest of cigarette smokers.
And he always knew where to get his thumbs on
the latest Playboy magazine.
He taught me the ways of the woods,
not the names of tree and wildflowers
but the cussing you could get away with on the trail.

His vital signs took no comfort
in the screen blips

and the tube floating from his arm.
I figured maybe broken windows,
carpet burns, crash-landing model airplanes,
would scare the crap out of an aneurysm.

He was lying in bed, silent and still,
surrounded by at least one pretty nurse
and two ultra-forgiving parents.
I wanted to burst out with,
"What have you got to complain about."
But I kept my tongue.
My biggest complaint, to this very day,
is with people who'd rather die than take it out on someone.

Regarding The Woman Across The Street

This poem is for the woman across the street.
She disliked doctors. And now the ambulance

is parked outside, red lights spinning.
And two rescue workers are inside her house

doing their best to keep her alive.
A heart attack, A stroke.

Neighborhood whispers bring her close to death.
My daughter catches my eye.

Her five year old, "What's happening?"
has no immediate answer.

Happening. You have to love the word.
It invokes something wild and free.

At least, it did back in the day.
This is more a case of "what's not happening?"

A body on a stretcher hauled out of a door
across the street will do that to you.

People have gathered. They're all doom-faced.
A lesson for my daughter I suppose

just in case she thought the world too pretty
with its garden flowers and lush summer trees.

No, despite the regalia of cherry blossoms
up and down the street,

the only paradise is a fool's one.
She will learn that soon enough.

But I can't get her away from the window.
For now, it fills her with light.

The sun's like a camera-man.
Hold it there. Keep it simple. It won't last.

He Falls In Love With A Painting

The wine and cheese party can go on without him.
He prefers to spend his time in another room,
admiring the painting above the mantle.
No glass in hand, no conversation he wishes to
share with anyone, he merely takes up
the best viewing distance to venerate
the fair-haired woman in white lace dress
posed lengthwise on the divan.
In his thoughts he is the one
who instructs her to sprawl a certain way,
with her head turned toward him,
lips slightly ajar, a third of the way to a smile.

He is the survivor of a half-dozen dead relationships.
A victim of loveliness that comes with a price.
But this is someone who will always be here
for him. She is motionless, a permanent revelation.
Come back ten years from now and nothing
will be different. She'll be on the verge of
unveiling a new face to him. He will respond with
the best of what he's capable of feeling.
Not knowing anything about the woman
is the perfect situation. Love and meditation
can interweave without interference from the
life's she's led. She's a flower the moment
of its blooming. Or his heart taking the purest stance.
Best of all, nothing is required but his presence.
Her role is unlimited and assured.

Welcome To The Whitehorse Inn

This is the Whitehorse,
a favorite drinking hole
of Dylan Thomas.
Come on in.
Have a whiskey.
Imagine it's the great Welsh bard's
seventh for the night.

Sit up at the bar.
Pretend he's on the stool beside you,
slurring words in an accent
as thick as his breath.
Just smile or nod in reply.
You're with Dylan Thomas.
Don't expect lines
of pure poetry.
Be content with a smelly belch.

So what if he's your hero.
Heroes don't spend all their lives
doing heroic things.
Sometimes, they prefer
to just drink themselves to death.
That's what makes them human.
And we only serve humans here.

Refugees

They're like a river looking for a sea,
an endless current of the displaced,
their course backed up,
turned around,
when they're not being yoked and tethered.

Everything's broken where they come from.
Every place along the way says "no."
By the time they reach the border,
nothing remains unsaid to them.
But for the gates. And the soldiers.
Faces rendered identical to the ones
who razed their village.

Here's where the stream
can push no further.
Hopelessly pressed against iron bars
is the very face of war.

October On Broad Street

Autumn in the inner city,
backyard trees,
even the rats that forage
in the lumps of leaves,
change color –
a stray dog figures he can chase those rodents
all the way back to Norway
but they laugh at him
by breeding more and more.

In a hollow under the house,
a groundhog digs himself in.
Boys, on knees,
seek him out with a flashlight.
Someone tosses a firecracker
in the direction of the den.
They're lucky the whole place doesn't burn.

Every oak and elm
drips like a leaky tap,
as the dead collect
between their roots,
or clog drains,
or take to the streets.

Insects die out.
Worms sleep.
The stray dog huddles in the doorway of a church.
"Make way, mutt," says a homeless man.

"That's my spot."
The dog's accommodating,
becomes a cold night's blanket.

Two kids see all this
from a second-floor tenement window.
This is the world
when nothing else is.

In My Dream

I was trapped in alley,
back flat against a stone wall.

Tanks rolled by
and soldiers patrolled the streets.

They barged into homes,
ransacked rooms,
interrogated family.

They halted traffic,
stopped men and women
on the sidewalk,
demanded their identity cards.

The locals gathered in angry groups,
noisy clusters shouting insults
at these invaders.

And, from a window,
an old woman spat
into the florid face
of a sergeant as he screamed,
"Where is he!"

Rumor scurried through the neighborhood
like rats.

They were looking for a poet.

I felt both terrified
and justified.

From Deep In The Bowels Of Suburbia

Anna and Jake split up.
She plays "World Of Warcraft" with some other guy now.
He sits at home
watching violent shows on cable TV.
Sometimes, Ally stops in on his way to clog-dancing.
They share a bong.
When the next MacArthur recipient awards are announced,
neither expect to be named.
Actually, the thing with Anna and the new guy
only lasted a month.
She's back with her mother.
They don't talk much.
At least not when it's time for America's Got Talent.
Jake is slowly weaning himself off WoW.
Grand Theft Auto is looking better by the night.
His Uncle Paul is serving ten years
for the real thing.
Jake is too lazy to follow in Paul's footsteps.
Paul always boasted, "No prison can hold me."
This one did.
His wife, Pamela filed for divorce when he was inside.
She married this muscleman who loves to high-five cops.
They have a kid, Archie, like in the comics,
who's into causes like Save the Whales.
When Paul was a kid, his dream was to work at the local Block-
buster.
But, then again, "Charlie's Angels" was his favorite movie.
Archie lives with his mother.
She and Ernie, the muscleman, make sure to speak softly

when they discuss her silicon implants.
Ernie is deathly afraid of genetically modified foods.
But he has no problem abusing OxyContin.
Archie has a girlfriend named Julie.
She works as a file clerk at the zoning commission.
Her father is an expert in voice-recognition software.
But when Julie calls him at work,
she has to explain, "Pop, this is me, Julie."

A Boy At The Wake

I was just a boy and there was no way
I could stay in the room with death.
No wonder I got fidgety.
No wonder I got dragged back
into that cruel, brutal wake,
not once but three times.

I longed for the moon, the stars,
that were just a flight of stairs,
an open door, away.
I was dressed in the kind
of suit I dreaded wearing
and the heavy curtains,
the moaning, the tears,
the low conversations that broke out
here and there,
were like more accessories
to my so-called Sunday best.

People die was the point
my parents were trying to put across.
Sometimes it's ones you love.
Sometimes, it's relatives
that you've maybe only met once or twice.
But you're of the same blood.
What they've got a lot of,
you share a little.

So I sat in a chair,
head down, feet scraping on the floor.
I pleaded with time to move faster
but it was as slow as the organ dirge
that played in the background.
I blocked my ears, as best I could,
to the pastor's canned sermon.

Some stranger came by,
looked at me
and said something to my parents like,
"My, how he's grown."
I'd been looking forward to growing up.
But the man in the box
up front, arrayed in flowers
was a warning of what could come of it.

Louisiana Childhood

He's out there among
the fireflies and the leaf hoppers,
grabbing at those pesky insects
as they zip by -
but always too late.

Or he's riding his bike
beyond his father's warnings,
to the edge of the swamp
where alligators bask
on floating islands
and mosquitoes go on a rampage
whenever they spy flesh.

Or he's somewhere in his yard
listening in on the conversations
between the grownups
on the front step.

Or he's cloistered in his room,
in summer heat,
sneaking a peek
at his older brother's skin mag.

Or he's in a parlor chair,
bent forward,
chin on palms,
engrossed in the action
on a black and white screen

that's so tiny, it's engulfed
by the console that surrounds it.

He knows nothing about
Rosa Parks or James Meredith
or Emmet Till or George Wallace
or Vietnam.
It's the Sixties
but with the Sixties shut out.

It's childhood.
It's an assignment
and he can't get out of it.

The Pleasure

It is revised downward by noisy spewing buses
and the dark roots of light hair.

Muzak takes its toll
as does mindless heavy metal.

Bugs modify its forest experience.
Bees sting from the depths of its honey.

It is rocked by earthquakes
and lesser phenomena like drizzly rain.

It is turned out by loud voices.
Must fend for itself when the people are obtuse.

Even inside the body it's not safe:
sour milk, aches and pains, bad memories.

Gravity does it no favors.
Not the way everything that rises falls.

The news is always out to get it.
What happens to other people happens to all.

And there's that feeling it can never be owned,
only borrowed. That's a killer.

It wants to give the impression that it's rare
and when it comes, I must make the most of it.

Such platitudes do it great harm.

Bathers

Bathers splash crazily in the turning tide
like they've just grabbed hold of faulty electrical wiring.
They're ridiculous in their simplicity.
And almost at a point where they can't imagine land.

How dull is the shore, and its assembly of self-worshipers.
No foam feathers, no big breaker suddenly going for its guns.
From towel after towel poke the toes that fear the water.
The sand is a perch for birds that never fly.

The Mississippi Above New Orleans

Towns look up at the Mississippi
from below the level of the sea,
breathe in its silt through lungs
that have to make do for gills.
There's nothing pure about these waters.
But memory never asks of time
that it see clear to the bottom.
And the river flows never far from a cemetery,
whose dead silently rejoice in the lapping.
Graves are not the anomalies they are elsewhere.
These are stray branches caught between rocks
or buried in the reeds.
The Mississippi sympathizes with spirits.
It too can move on
and yet be left behind the times.
Never does flowing water seem so stagnant,
an illusion blessed by
green moss on stones,
fading French names
carved into the steamy, fragrant air of dusk.
A boat idles by,
Despite the putt-putt of its engine,
and flanks of moldy wood,
it achieves grace
like all do as they skim the surface.
Even the mallards.
Even a stray pelican blown up from the delta.
The Mississippi settles in its flow, rich and sustaining
It meanders through the lively and the doomed.

It would love to show you the gold
but the upstream dross will have to do.
And it inevitably obeys the first law of rivers.
Do as the map tells you.
And then more.

Emma

In a man's deep eyes, how empty the craters.
Heart, give me the exact moment. All other times fall flat.
The first drop confused you. You survived. But then there was
the second.
Yeah, good old diesel train. The ghost of steam is in fine hands.

This is a God-like wind, otherwise why all the regret, the phony
repentance.
And that's a wonderful crackle of dead leaves underfoot. Of
death anywhere.
Dear friends - the internet being so insatiably digital, I'm just a
human blob.
If you could only see my solitude. My jealousies almost sob.

In this keyboard, I have discovered an ancient treasure map.
The x says, what is death but the lengthy kiss of bone and air.
I type nothing. The lack of words is my contribution. The lack of
meaning is God's.
In anything, the very core is you. Here or not here. Take that as
a complement.

It's not pretty - the last of what we are. It wasn't meant to be.
The awkward guy, left of frame, that's me. The center? A
vacuum now.
The limp puff of the damp cigarette or the clogged chimney. Me again.
What a house I live in. Love left and it was the same as me staying.

Intruder In The Mist

Darkness holds up its mirror. My harsh reflection
Accentuates how much the parting day conceals,
But evening, for all its stone-blindness, reveals;
The true face within, malevolent complexion
Suspended in ebony, a dire confection
Of harpy, leech, demon, monster, the grim ordeals
Of knowing the beast that I really am. It seals
My soul for foulness, predation and infection.

Dank air, gathering mist, nothing to reassure
Potential prey, whose unwitting presence completes
My nefarious task, my trail interwoven
With bat-wing flicker, spider web and serpent spoor
As I haunt the coarse bedraggled moonless back streets
With evil's night eye and a foot part-way cloven.

The Rounds

Doctor and nurse
are in close conversation
out of patient's earshot
Their feelings for each other
are not under discussion.
Nor is the weather.
Or the strange car
in his reserved spot
that morning.
It's all to do with charts.
They stare at them
as if they're archaeologists
confronted by hieroglyphics.
But then comes the head nodding.
The doctor starts it.
She follows through with
a less pronounced arching of the neck,
bobbing of the chin.
"I'm increasing his dosage to..."
That's what the old man hears.
All he takes away from it is that
whatever it is that's doing his
insides no good, then he's
getting more of it.
And it's in Latin besides.
It annoys him when
he's nothing more than tense whispers.
It's like footsteps on his grave
and he's not even dead yet.

He's got suffering enough
without Bat-doc and Robin-nurse inflicting more.
There's this jabbing pain in his groin
like he's being knifed.
Some midgets are playing baseball in his head.
And his chest is as tight
as his Scottish grandfather.
But then the doctor turns towards him.
His smile is right out of
"Emily Post's Guide To Bedside Manner."
"So how are we this morning?" he asks.
The old man resists the urge to say,
"You tell me."
Sick as he feels,
he still prefers his own version of events.

An Education In The Northern Woods

The endless canopy is long since broken
and yet, there remains these vast stretches
of northern New England,
outside the boundaries of our consciousness,
where time is dense and heavy, moves slow,
and size doesn't factor in humanity.

I stand at the base of a red oak, a willing dwarf,
stare up at branches lofty enough to be sky.
Light perforates the summery cover with
bright lances, shimmering arrows.

My son is farther ahead,
lured by the sirens of a nearby stream.
While he stirs the waters,
I struggle to look down to the bottom.
Is that a cross half-buried in the silt or just a stone?
He's a succession of disparate noises,
excitement packaged in sapling skin and bone.
How cruel he is to the gentle cadence of this place.
Shush I say, like a haughty librarian,
but that doesn't stop the babbling.

He wants to step out on the slippery rocks
or scramble up the swamp oak.
Fan-shaped orange chicken mushrooms hold no interest.
Nor polypore wedged like upside down saucers in a birch.
I try to hold him back with a darner
buzzing on a branch, its abdomen sheer and blue as opal.

But my son rattles on as if this is a schoolyard
and I am a dozen of his friends.

He doesn't understand that this world calls for silence, stillness -
like maidenhair, shuffled by wind but rooted in place,
scalloped edge of fronds tickling the nearest maple trunk.

Two hundred years ago, I tell him,
this was all farms.
And now eastern red cedar grazes,
scotch pine sheds its needles on cornfield bones.
The kid's as antsy as a chipmunk.
It's not that the woods bore him.
But he's young and one place at a time
is three too few.

He can't rest on a fallen log
or drop to his knees,
stick his nose in the trillium's jaw.
He doesn't understand that once this was all there was.
Look around. If this foliage, the wildlife,
couldn't house and feed you
then you'd crawl up under a willow tree and die.

It's the primitive, the remote,
that I wish to enter into
but he holds me back with fear of a failing grade,
or dislike of an assigned chore
or the latest joke relayed around his classroom.

He can't leave behind what he knows of life.
This is all new to him
but it's not an alternative,

merely something to be added on
to what he has already accumulated.

I seek out peace and understanding
beyond my own cocoon,
in the heron footprints on the muddy pond banks,
the juice from the downy gray milkweed leaf,
the flashy calico pennant and flashing lightning bug,
a flurry of cabbage whites like rising snow.

If only he would tire,
seek rest and shelter, stay still, absorb.
If only we could flop somewhere on the ground together,
enrapt in the. meadow-around us,
its hush broken only by the call of an unseen bird,
the buzz, the flicker of insects making their brief living.

That's the way to a proper education.
Whatever the lesson,
it is all to the good
and not coming from inside us...until it is.

The Loneliest Man In The World

Nobody knows me here.
No friends.
I'm totally alone.
Then you call.

My voice is trembling.
Haven't spoken to
anyone in days
and even then
it was a wrong number.
The woman asked for Mavis.
I was terrified
from not being the woman
she was looking for.

What does a guy say
when he has nothing to say?
You sound strong
and I feel weak.
You make a point.
It feels like a decimal
pressing hard
against my brow.
You're also looking
for Mavis.

It's a Mavis world
and she's not even in it.

Passive Anger

I confess I once jerked a flower
from out of her precious garden,
stripped it of petals,
snapped the stem,
and all right before her eyes.

It was all the violence I
was capable of
The thought of lashing out physically
at another human being sickened me.
And I had great respect
for the animal kingdom
down to its most minimalist ant.
And as for throwing things -
one inanimate object against another.
That's always leads to breakage,
and loud noise.

So instead, I made my unhappiness known
by killing something that I knew
would regrow itself in that very same spot,
be just as beautiful and intoxicatingly scented
as its predecessor.

Besides, she was going to prune the thing anyway,
For a healthier garden, she said.
Like our brief disagreement.
it was sudden, emotional, necessary
for the health of all.

It just didn't get to live out its last days
in a vase that's all.
Yes, the vase -
that thing I picked up
but then put down gently.

The Phony Thaw

An emboldened sun
is still a puny one.
A brief attempt to win over
the hearts of February
fools a garden,
deceives a bank of crocuses,
some credulous asters,
with its temperature conjuring trick.
Insects' coded instructions
are lost in translation.
They uncork like a wine bottle.
Even the spider,
half-hibernating in a barn recess,
weaves its white-mesh canopy
into the encouraging light.
Birds forgo the truth of the calendar.
fill the lie with song.
A depleted oak,
its buds barely grazing the surface
of its branches,
awakens to a reverent choir of sparrows.
And where is winter in all of this?
Deep in the woods, plotting?
At the heart of a dripping icicle
planning a frozen way back?
A wildflower pokes its head up through
a thatch of brown grass.
French aristocrats were guillotined for less.

Between The Woman And The Telemarketer

Hold the phone.
There's a woman in the garden.
I can't talk right now.
I'm too busy being in love.
Sun's like a spotlight
Iris and rose are audience.
There's no breeze
yet still their petals clap.

Go about your business, telemarketer.
Find someone else to bother,
a poor soul
without a window to his back yard,
and an angel on her knees
with pruning shears,
a bed of flowers aching to be clipped.

Truly, a head bowed into
the reds, the yellows, the greens,
is so much more
than a lifetime subscription
to whatever it is you're selling.

She's troweling open the earth.
Can your magazines or
identity protection or
timeshare in Saint Maarten do that?

Colors pop in her lovely fingers.
Your salesmanship cannot compare.
My eyes, my mouth, my whole body,
is lining up for her delicate attention.

Listen for a moment to what I'm selling:
what you need is not a pigeon
but a lover of your own.

The next click you hear
will be my best offer.

The Farm-Woman

It's not the same.
Sunset is too organized.
The flame rising in the night
is a show for businessmen's children.
The true fire is no more.
The light is merely wind-blown ashes.

She outlived her husband and her strength,
moved into town, first a small apartment,
then a nursing home.
Saying goodbye to her made me wince.
I couldn't sense anything in her
to convince me she wouldn't be dead tomorrow.

I remember a land of endless yellow patches,
the color closest to brightness.
From a plane above,
passengers could see the artistry of farmers at work,
a fabulous quilt, two hundred miles wide, a hundred across.
For years, steadily, through the best and worst weather,
from lush times to when drought had no answers –
quilt was a good name for it.
It kept tired people safe and warm.

She'd often sigh how a way of life was dying.
And now I drive by the old place,
and am dismayed by all the corporate tractors
giving burial their best shot.
Progress is merciless. Her fears have come to be.

Driving by siloes huge as moon rockets,
bigger but fewer towns,
simple gifts turned to big paydays,
I have visions of the edges of her mouth,
smiling out of habit
and the glow of her wrinkled eyes,
stubborn in her suffering:
It pains me to think
that nothing good came of that

Dream Woman/Dream Man

Dream woman does a number on her real counterpart.
It gets to the point where flesh and blood
is no longer the standard for existence.
You come to realize that only the dream woman
can satisfy the most unspoken of your desires.
The real woman is merely a compendium of faults,
ordinariness and tasks that need to be done.
Yes, she gets under the sheets with you,
you dine together, and she shares your walks
through the woods, those drives into the country.
But, in none of these moments, does she realize
that you already have company.
And then when she's doing something mundane
like grocery shopping or laundry,
you really do have dream woman all to yourself.
The problem is that there's nothing to stop
your real woman having her own dream man.
And no way you'd want to stack your virtues up against his.
His attentions would be unwavering, his touch persuasive.
He'd say everything she wanted to hear
as if she had written him a script.
No matter where she was, he'd be in immediate contact with her life.
You figure it's already happened,
that she's imagined this Adonis into being.
For you catch her smiling when she irons, singing as she scrubs
the floor.
You don't introduce your dream woman to her.
She's equally reticent regarding her dream man.
What happens is, the two dream lovers become aware of each other.

More than that, it's adoration at first sight.
They elope, leaving behind two real people.
The shared experience becomes a kind of self-serving love.
You don't discuss how you've been jilted, betrayed.
You defer to a kind of dream silence, the most real silence of all.

The Crystal Horse

She refers to it as a collectible.
It's a horse made of crystal
that has sat on her bedroom dressing table
for as long as she's been a woman.

She wipes it clean every day
and makes sure it's placed exactly
where the light falls,
turns it into sparkling diamonds.

Once, she caught a nephew handling it
and she would have throttled the boy
if her brother hadn't intervened.

It's the one thing she claims as valuable.
And that treasure is for no one's hands but her own,
The family, even the newest generation,
know better than to venture anywhere near
Aunt's Jemma's twinkling horse.

Now in her eighties,
she's struggling with arthritis
and the quandary of whether or not
she ought to have a will drawn up.

She would die intestate
if it weren't for that crystal horse.
She wants to provide for its future,
not have it lumped in

with her quilts and cutlery,
the kitchen table and the microwave.

It could be stashed in a drawer.
Or stuck on a mantle
where it would only gather dust.
She has no faith in anyone in the family.
It might never glisten again.
That's why she's still living.
She doesn't trust death with the light.

My Connection

The plane departs late.
And it spends an hour or more
circling Washington airport
awaiting an okay to land.
Meanwhile, I'm in my seat,
squashing the empty peanut packet,
cursing, under my breath,
everything from the pilot,
to air traffic control, to time,
to the nation's capital,
to the woman in the seat beside me
who's been all the flight
working on the one Sudoku problem.
Finally, we touch down.
I have a half hour to make my connection.
I've no idea what terminal
it's taking off from.
The airport's so huge,
gate D47 could be in Delaware
for all I know.
And then we taxi
like we're stuck in Times Square traffic.
And the idiots deplaning in front of me
move like snails in a heat wave.
Finally, I get off that damn aircraft
and begin what amounts to a marathon
but at a sprinter's speed.
I do my best Usain Bolt imitation
up the escalators,

outrun the moving sidewalk,
pace up and down in
the inter-terminal subway car,
burst through its sliding doors
like a quarter-horse,
then slalom through crowds,
at high speed, to my gate
wave my boarding pass at the scanner
before my final lap down to the tunnel,
into the jet, to seat 26A,
the only empty,
strap in,
then let out a sigh
long and loud to be heard
through the first-class curtains.
Skip ahead six hours,
and I'm kissing and hugging you
like I've been on Shackleton's
Antarctic expedition
and not a two-week business trip.
Meanwhile, every other guy
who could have been hugging
and kissing you
either missed their next flight,
or had engine trouble
or a three-hour layover,
or trotted when they
should have galloped.
There were even a few
who made it with me this far.
But those dumb fools are now
hugging and kissing other women.

Catalogues

Catalogues arrive in droves.
They want me fitted out with hunting rifles,
fishing waders up to my knees.
They'd have me listen to
CD's of the Four Lads
or take home courses in Philosophy.
Some even think I'm Joan not John.
Hence, I'm let into the secrets
of somebody called Victoria.

I've heard this is all very scientific,
that my purchases tell the world about me,
trigger a response in various points of the compass
that automatically sends a glossy brochure
directly to my house.

I confess I abhor shopping.
Unless I'm wading through piles
of second hand books of course.
And now the enemy thinks it's doing me a favor
by laying me to siege
though my traitorous mailbox.
Every one of these catalogues goes
directly into the trash.
As I do it,
I imagine I'm some goliath
dumping a chain store
into the abyss.

It's a commercial world so they tell me.
A catalogue is capitalism's advanced guard.
They know I'm in here.
But they don't know me.

On The Walk To Marge's After Henry's Death

My wife and I walk slowly,
and not just because of the ice.
We're praying for that pace that never gets us there.
And we can feel the winter chill
jabbing at our bones.
But it will seem good-natured
up against the biting cold of death.

"He was old," my wife says.
She may as well declare
that death is the cure for cancer.

I can imagine the scene when
we get there, tea and cookies
on a tray in a parlor with floral drapes,
Marge anxious to serve to
the two of us seated on a brown sofa with
cushions for our elbows.
For ten minutes or more, none of us
will even mention Henry.
She'll pour, we'll sip, we'll nibble.
And then my wife will volunteer,
"Is there anything we can do?"
And Marge will burst into tears.

I hate that prospect and my legs know it.
Why can't I slip. Why not a broken bone.
Why not my wife's tears as she drags me back home

to the safety of everyone in the house alive and well.
But no, we have sympathy to perform,
and to do it properly, we have to be there.
Words so sad, so heavy, they'll stay around
longer than Henry did.
Maybe if it wasn't winter.
But what other season could it be.
Clouds are gray overhead but it still won't snow.
No flake wants to land on Marge's roof.
It might never leave.

The Artist In The Moment

He's as precise as a moment.
The one where loft shadows
get it just right. And dust motes
thread the skylight shine. And
her face must not merely trace
that fine line between plain and beauty,
it must be that line.

It's more than just a model holding still,
the world must also comply.
The air needs to crest, her surrounds
be at the point of forcing the issue.
His palette stiffens in a tensed wrist
as if holding a scene taut.
The supple brush flickers in its gates
like a sprinter.

Only he knows perfect.
So he sharpens his senses
as objects defer their own perceptions
to the eye that caters to his sensibility.

Then like a twitch in a left thumb,
like an eyebrow tilt,
the twist of a nerve down his excited arm,
it is there, he paints so briefly, and then it's gone.

"Same time tomorrow," he tells her.
He already knows the finished painting.
Everything else has yet to learn.

Looking West From My Sister's Property In Emerald

There's all this sameness for my eyes to waste,
red clay, thin top soil, rocky dunes like ocean waves,
all abandoned here by searing sun's rays,
to be rolled up like a carpet by the night.

So arid, water is the most Christian of the virtues,
tapped from the underground artesian sea,
pumped by pipe and windmill's muscle,
to calm and make something of the rippling sands.

For even in deprivation, there is presence to make known,
surprising resources of determination and survival,
of weather watch and jutted jawline,
that makes my own resilience jealous.

So many reminders here of my inner dust,
the casual breeze swirling the surroundings slow,
making a shadow, not of my body, but of my life,
and a land equal part everything and nothing to do with me.

The Bet

This is not like a garden,
not a simple matter of planting seeds,
watering, fertilizing,
and leaving time and weather to do the rest.

Besides the hardscrabble
of the daily feeding,
weary hugs at two in the morning,
nurturing, watching over
like an eagle with a chick,

it's a bet you place
at a random totalizer,
a wager that you'll be here in twenty two years
for the graduation
or twenty six for the wedding
and maybe thirty years
for the first grandchild.

It's not just a flutter.
You bet the future
without even looking at the odds.
And, more than that,
it's a parlay,
that throws in your child
and your child's child
and every generation to come.

So few horses running a race
against all that can happen in this world.
And maybe a finish line out there somewhere.
Be grateful if you can't see it.

Those Times She Really Does Need You

It is infuriating I am sure
but there comes a time
when you must drop this business
of your business,
and reach out your hand,
like there's a paint-brush in it
and instead of pushing
all the buttons
in your cash register of a lover
you must dapple something in
those gaps in her color
a touch of texture,
a dream, a promise, if you will.

It must be hard always
being in your body
with its constant bulletins,
its faxes, e-mails,
from the hard sell
of the present
when it's the timeless gestures
that are suddenly required,
when a tear jams the gears,
a crooked smile
abends the program,
a desperate cry from another's throat
wipes away, in an instant,
the proud prospectus
of many profitable years.

From speeches to underlings
to the soothing of another,
the tongue can clamber up and down
some treacherous steps.
There is one broken stair
for the lecture
brittle of bone
and nervous underfoot
but there is one smooth
and supporting stair
for the face
kissed flush against the moonlight,
pinning it to
the solution of the stars.

With An Ex, This Is As Good As It Gets

Across the table from you,
I'm at my most emotionless,
speaking of mundane matters
in short sentences,
as if my life now
is barely worth repeating.

Your voice is soft
but equally unobtrusive.
You reduce your life
to some kind of DIY kit
that you put together
in your spare time.

I try to recollect
but tender moments
are buried in the rubble
of intervening years.

And you do tap a little
on your memories,
but nostalgia won't come
to the door.

And yet it's good to see you.
And you say that it's good to see me.
We make no plans to meet up again.
That's even better.

Coincidentally

I'm a man
but it was a close run thing.
I could have been a woman.
Not sure what my name would have been:
Joanne. Jenna.
The possibilities are endless
and far from benign.

As a man,
various motives and movements
have brought me to this place
I occupy today.
Nothing went according to plan.
Some choices were third, fourth or fifth options.
Others weren't choices at all.

Take heed.
When I was younger,
there was every chance that alcohol would decide my fate.
Booze has a language all its own.
I spoke it on many occasions.
Luckily, no woman believed me.
Then I got sober,
what I used to refer to as
the day the world ended.

Had I been a woman
I might have got pregnant and not known who the father was.

Of course, my boy could have grown up to be president.
Or a poet at least.

But I'm a man
and I married a woman.
A series of coincidences brought us together.
But such accidents, flukes, are not unknown
on the busy streets, workplaces, neighborhoods,
I which I live.

In fact, humanity is organized into coincidences.
Like the fact that I'm a man and not a woman.
And I have a wife, not a husband.
On my wedding day, the world came back from the dead.
I drank a toast and another and another.
I got so drunk, I forgot what sex I was.

My First And Last Time Hunting

I obeyed Jack's instructions,
knelt in the damp grass,
under cover of a giant pine,
hidden from the direction of the wind.
A white-tail buck feasted
at the rim of the forest and glade,
ten-pointer, proud, the angle
of his head never deviating
from the line of that ridge
of brown backbone,
but cautious, nervous, his meal,
a mix of nibbling and sniffing.

My uncle fondled gun metal
like a mistress.
He caressed, coaxed its flash handle,
long barrel, tickled that trigger
as if there were more life
in weapon than beast.
For a moment that was true.
The shot rang out.
The deer fell silent
and the gun kept talking,
loud and drunk with smoke.

He strapped his prize
to the roof of the truck,
blood brown by this
and sticking to the wound.

All the way home,
those horns scraped their spoor
in the fading paint.
Jack didn't like venison.
dumped the now headless carcass on a friend.
He didn't like me much either,
informed my mother,
"well at least he kept quiet."

Now, if someone mentions hunting,
I'm not so quiet.

Dirge

There is no organ, merely the sound of it in my head.
And whoever's playing never strays from the low notes.
Dirige, Domine, Deus meus, in conspectus tuo viam meam.
My thoughts forgo translation. There's no need.

The world resembles a funeral home.
The curtains are white, not deep purple,
but the lack of human footprint is the same in both cases.
It's not as if I'm mourning. I've become mourning itself.

Feel free to use me if your sorrows aren't cavernous enough.
Yes, it's winter, but my insides rolled out the season months ago.
They took the phone calls. They read the newspapers.
They attended the bedsides. They stood out in cemetery rain.

My expression was brave throughout
but my feelings finetuned to the darkest timbre.
No, there is no organ. My body can't contain such an instrument.
But pedalboards pump somber wind. Senses respond in kind.

I am a font of music downcast but not downplayed.
Living among people demands I give it my attention.
And there is only one way this song will ever stop.
To Brig O'Dread thou comst at last.

The Map Man

He could read all kinds of topographic maps,
and spoke at least five languages.
He dressed well, if a little behind the times,
and his hands were smooth, his voice lilting,
and his shoes as polished as a general's.

He didn't laugh loudly, preferring a polite chuckle.
And was no drinker, save for the occasional glass of port.

What he did for a living was mostly rumors.
Some said he was a nuclear scientist.
Others figured him for a spy.
But he gave no indication of either.
Except, from time to time, he'd been seen
doing what looked like lip-reading
a conversation across the room.

He lived alone in one of the new townhouses.
No one ever saw him with a woman,
just the occasional male friend
in a fancy wine bar.
The maps would be spread out on the table.
And someone once overheard
what sounded like German or even French,
as he pointed at various brown contours,
bright blue lakes and rivers.
Maybe he's planning an invasion,
was one old guy's suggestion.

He was a local mystery,
one desperately needed,
for knowing everybody else's business
could only take a person's boredom so far.
Folks would stop and stare
when they saw him out and about.
If not for him,
they never would have wondered.

Newspapers

People are such crap is what you're trying to tell me.
Mastodons or cobras or stinking pits of offal.
A barbarian wants my vote. A wax dummy is
trying to sell me something. And shares in spit
will be the next big thing.

Forty dead by page seven and weather only
accountable for nine. Jail terms handed out
like medals. Gangsters teach school. Celebrities
start churches. Two muscle men scrap in a ring
and the crowd goes wild.

So what's the score? Drought. Pestilence.
War. A million starving. When do I get
to pick my fantasy Africa team? Louts
write editorials. The asinine agree. Three
journalists were shot. Two would like to be.

And, on page thirty, local news, the village
idiot now runs the village. The town cop shot
and killed his wife, arrested himself, went up
before his brother the judge, is now out on
parole. And the Chinese just purchased the Niagara Falls.

I'm weary by the time I reach the deaths of
ordinary people. The one time they get their picture
in the paper they don't get to see it. But if a saber tooth
tiger dies. Or the head hog. Now that's a different story.
No, it's the same story. But with a bigger byline.

The classifieds... man who hates women seeks woman
who hates men. The comics... laugh and you laugh
at a guy blowing out his brains, fifteen hookers in a paddy
wagon. And lastly, the horoscope. Today is a bad day to
read newspapers. Other than that, you're good to go.

Children Lost In The Woods

Lost in the woods for almost a year,
they've turned themselves into bark or lichen.
And thick brush. And long grass. And scat.

They no longer worry when the dark clouds move in.
In fact, they welcome the rain.
And are happy to blow in the fiercest wind.
Or dine with the soil below.

They welcome birdlife with natural bonhomie.
And the stars as comrades in fire.
They no longer speak.
What they are speaks for them.

Keep looking if you must.
But what's in plain sight
defies finding.

No tiny gripping hands.
Their reach is wide.
No laughter, no tears.
Just growth and running water.

And they are all colors now
not just the clothes they were wearing.

The Other Person

It's not the street lamp
but its fragile voice,
nor the sidewalk,
just the winds it broadcasts.
A woman has no better place to be.
That's the tongue-less language hereabouts.
And it's not the city.
The hot dog swimming in blood
is the city
The taxi and its clunky meter,
its neon yellow doors,
is the city.
It's what floats above the city
even as it seems to rise up
from below.
A woman is someone called Elizabeth
who you cannot know.
Lizzie's eyes look carved out of her skull.
They can stare a shadow down.
And it sure isn't the room she takes you to,
not that creaking flight of stairs,
And forget the bed.
That's the mattress
where life and death fought
and sex won.
Sure she undresses
but not down to anything.
She holds you like she holds her money.
But only one is stashed into her purse.

So what do you have for evidence?
A kiss that leaks from her lips
like horsehair from a blanket.
A hand-job like she's swatting flies.
Something called penetration
which is nothing but smelly water
sloshing down a sewer pipe.
The pillow is a rock.
The blanket is a road-sign.
And the woman is a woman?
Can anything be what you say it is.

Abduction

The school bus has been sighted in the area.
Kids stand on sidewalks in the cold,
some with a parent, some alone.

Red lights flash. Doors creak open.
A monitor waves children aboard.
Traffic stops in both directions.

Soon there's no kids to be seen anywhere
and cars can now move freely.
If anything else came through the neighborhood

scooped up the coming generation,
drove off to who knows where,
the heart would be torn out of the houses.

But people make allowances for education.
It abducts one child, returns one child.
The hope is that they not be the same.

The Dead Of Oz

Many small mounds
on a hill
overlooking
the yellow brick road –

in a makeshift mausoleum,
a pile of tin,
a heap of straw
and a lion skin –

a large stone cross
making the spot
where the good witch Glinda
is buried –

two graves
unmarked but for the words
'east' and 'west' –

a glowing neon sign
announcing,
"here lies the great wizard" -

the bones of a young girl
and her dog,
with the epitaph,
"Not in Kansas anymore –
not in Oz either."

Welcome To The Natural World

Shrunken heart, in a tiny kitchen,
you're long past the season of your youth,
You find your solace only in the obituaries,
or the cold that has everyone bundled up
and not just you and your pacemaker.
Hardened arteries, blotchy skin -
how can this ever be the way forward.
No encouragement from your veins.
It's all they can do to make it to your surfaces.
Your body struggles to the parlor.
Like it or not, the only action is on the television.
Your senses gravitate to nature programs.
A lioness stalks a herd of zebra.
You sympathize with that black and white striped horse.
But it's the feline that strikes the jealous note.
If only you could move with such cruel elegance.
But your bones creak like snapping chalk.
And you cough like an old charcoal fire.
Your prey would feel your presence from a mile away.
The camera moves in for a close-up
as the lioness leaps upon the zebra's back.
It's an uneven contest.
Of course, in your life, contests always are.
Then there's scenes of the male and two cubs
feasting on the kill.
You'd look away but your neck muscles forbid.
Up next is the mandatory scene
of that lazy full-maned lout mounting
the one that's done all the work.
A smile of recognition crosses your lips.

People Are No Good

They get cancer.
They forget your birthday.
They run you off the road.
They die.

Look around.
Each one of the people you see
is capable of such harm.

They sue you.
They fall out of love with you.
They put down your favorite song.
They don't want to know you.

It's not cats I'm talking about.
It's not squirrels.
And it's sure not inanimate things
like rocks and fences.

Except people run over cats.
And they shoot squirrels.
And they throw rocks.
And they put up those damn fences.

Maybe it's not even their fault.
Could be that there's something
inherent in people
that the best they can do
is harm you in some way.

They earn more money.
They drive fancier cars.
They live in bigger houses
in better neighborhoods.

People can do damage
just by being who they are.
And I'm who I am.
It's just not working out.

Regarding Love

Love is as fundamental to the human condition
as the five senses.

The need for love is as basic as the need for
a quarter-pounder with cheese at McDonalds.
Perhaps even more so.

Without fast food, one dies of good nutrition.

But, without love, sight, touch, taste, smell, hearing
are like those tiny packets of condiments…
unused, discarded, for there is no meal.

Ella

I still have
the record album
she left behind
though I haven't
seen her in years.

I play it
from time to time.
I think of her
now and again.

Do them both together
and I run the risk
of dancing.

Frogs

So many frogs leaping across the wet field,
it doesn't occur to me to catch one.
I had the one father, and that one,
that uniqueness made it a large number
even as I knew, the frogs were merely
something disassembled, tiny hopping
pieces of the master frog, so spread
out across the soggy earth, there's no
way I could get them back together,
no way to know them whole.
But my father, being one, even when shrinking,
even when the skeleton he became
threatened to rob my sight of him,
there was no sense of him splitting apart.
Though emaciated, he kept it all.

I had kept a frog once, kidnapped it
from its pond, stored it in a bottle
with nail-pricked lid to give it air.
Didn't know then that it needed more
than short bouts of my curious face
through glass to sustain it.
Didn't appreciate that whatever is separated
from the tribe of itself
cannot be enough of a thing to survive.

Always struggled to be whole, to be inclusive.
Sure, there's tears but only to protect the eye.
Even bending down at his side

when he could have pulled some of me into death^
I kept myself together.
Outside, grayer and rainier
than it should be for August,
an invasion of frogs, if we only knew.
And nothing I could do,
short of dying with him

A Trial Separation On Trial

I'm still not clear on how it happened.
Or even where.
Sure, there's people not happy about it
but their ranks have thinned over the years.
What's that you say?
Sorry, I can't hear.
My ear's in mothballs.
And please don't scream.
You'll wake the baby.
Of course, there is no baby.
No mother either.
I'm so alone, I could die in my pajamas,
staring into the fog of death, mistaking it for sleep.
That's me.
Always on the cusp of life and death.
A study in Hermeneutics and predestination.
Cross my o's, dot my t's,
before truth and method get here.
And suddenly a phone call from out of the blue
rings like smoke spirals rising from a cigarette
Wrong number? Forgiveness?
Forgiveness but still a wrong number?
Who can bear these oblivious distances,
people standing in their bright tropical garb
while I am huddled up in the chill off my own body?
It is she, says the voice.
It is she but without the urgency.

She sounds calm as if nothing ever happened.
But everything's happened.
If not, why am I in such
advanced stages of myself?

Splendor

Beak to beak,
a bright red cardinal is feeding
his brown bride.
Gloom turns to sprinkle,
but the birds
don't seem to notice.
We watch instinctively,
drawn by the colors
and the love.
Drizzle forms a curtain around all,
a luminous quiet,
a splendid seclusion.

The Future Of Literature

In this bookstore,
the classics are squeezed between
Sports and Dogs.
It's Jay Gatsby versus Tom Buchanan
over fifteen rounds
for the championship of the 1920's.
And under the tree
from a "Child's Christmas In Wales"
yelps an anxious Corgi puppy.
Rob Roy's pitching
and David Copperfield is catching,
Giant St Bernards
lumber up the snowy Alps
to rescue Lorna from the evil Doones.
Uncle Tom is on the ten yard line
and threatening to score.
Flat-faced Pekes
adorn the laps of Austen heroines.
But soon enough,
even the little shelf space
occupied by masterworks
will be too much.
Self-help books encroach.
Best sellers need more room to grow.
What's left for Macbeth
after he's learned to win friends and influence people?
And poor Josef K.
If the law courts weren't convoluted enough,
here comes the "Da Vinci Code."

Eventually, the great novels of the past
will be things of the past.
But not in the Nostalgia section.
That's for traditional recipe cookbooks.
Or old comic book price guides.
Dracula's nightly feasting won't include
his grandmother's goulash.
Poor d'Artagnan will never regret
tossing his childhood Spiderman collection.
Such is the future of literature.
The lost world won't ever be found.
The invisible man will stay that way.

ACKNOWLEDGEMENTS

Biomath — North Dakota Quarterly

My Complaint Department — Beechwood Review
Regarding The Woman Across The Street — Willard And Maple
He Falls In Love With A Painting — Willard And Maple
Welcome To The Whitehorse Inn — Studio One
Refugees — Nebo
October On Broad Street — Evening Street Review

In My Dream — Washington Square Review

Message To Mary — Liquid Imagination
From Deep In The Bowels Of Suburbia — Ellipsis
Louisiana Childhood — Havik
A Boy At The Wake — Floyd County Moonshine

The Pleasure — Abbey
Bathers — Blue Unicorn
The Mississippi Above New Orleans — Down To The Dark River

Emma — Eunoia Review
Intruder In The Midst — Hedge Apple Halloween Special

The Rounds — Blood And Thunder
An Education In The Northern Woods — Riverrun
The Loneliest Man In The World — Hawaii Pacific Review

Passive Anger — Slab
The Phony Thaw — Icon

Between The Woman And The Telemarketer	That Literary Review
The Farm-Woman	Studio One
Dream Woman/Dream Man	Obsessed With Pipework
The Crystal Horse	Front Range Review
My Connection	Brushfire
On The Walk To Marge's After Henry's Death	White Wall Review
Catalogues	Elm Leaves Journal
The Artist In The Moment	Rockhurst Review
Looking West From My Sister's Property In Emerald.	New Croton Review
The Bet	Old Red Kimono
Those Times She Really Does Need You	Inscape
With An Ex, This Is As Good As It Gets	Third Wednesday
Coincidentally	Floyd County Moonshine
My First And Last Time Hunting	Rathalla Review
Dirge	Compose
The Map Man	Chronogram
Newspapers	Canyon Voices
Children Lost In The Woods	International Poetry Review
The Other Person	Eunoia Review
Abduction	Ship Of Fools
Welcome To The Natural World	Slant
People Are No Good	Nebo
Regarding Love	Nebo
Ella	Drabble
Frogs	Poet Lore

A Trial Separation On Trial	Modern Poetry Review
Splendor	Highland Park Poetry
The Future Of Literature	Voices De La Luna
Poetry Lesson 1	Bond Street Review
The Hurt Does Not Inspire Me To Write	Woodcrest Magazine
The Voices	Redactions
His Floaters	Misfit
Between Two Fires	Inscape
The End Of A Perfect Relationship	Canyon Voices
A Man's Sleep Is No Longer Hos Castle	Metonym
After The Forest Fire	Front Range Review